OSCAR
by my side

*The Story of a Tiny Dachshund and
the Girl Who Loved the Sea*

Linda Atkinson

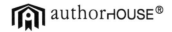 authorHOUSE®

AuthorHouse™ LLC
1663 Liberty Drive
Bloomington, IN 47403
www.authorhouse.com
Phone: 1-800-839-8640

Published by AuthorHouse 02/21/2014

ISBN: 978-1-4918-5701-4 (sc)
ISBN: 978-1-4918-5700-7 (e)

Library of Congress Control Number: 2014901265

Any people depicted in stock imagery provided by Thinkstock are models, and such images are being used for illustrative purposes only. Certain stock imagery © Thinkstock.

Because of the dynamic nature of the Internet, any web addresses or links contained in this book may have changed since publication and may no longer be valid. The views expressed in this work are solely those of the author and do not necessarily reflect the views of the publisher, and the publisher hereby disclaims any responsibility for them.

Acknowledgements

I would like to thank the "actual" Oscar and Rita (Rachel), whose unconventional adventures filled the pages of my journal for almost two years; ultimately evolving into, *OSCAR BY MY SIDE...The Story Of A Tiny Dachshund And The Girl Who Loved The Sea.*

I would be remiss without mentioning the renowned British author and veterinarian, James Herriot. He was my favorite childhood author, and his books fascinated and inspired me with his remarkable accounts of being a country veterinarian in England and Scotland.

In his celebrated book, *All Things Bright and Beautiful,* you can find this lovely quote:

> *All things bright and beautiful,*
> *All creatures great and small,*
> *All things wise and wonderful,*
> *The Lord God make them all.*
> Cecil Frances Alexander 1818-1895

Dedication

I dedicate this book to all the wonderful and caring people who have found their way to animal shelters, and adopted loving and faithful companions for themselves or for their children.

Growing up as an only child, my rescued pets brought me friendship and taught me responsibility, but most of all I discovered unconditional love from each and every one of those precious animals.

"THANK YOU," to all of you who care! You have saved a life, ended suffering, and have given **yourself** the gift of "unconditional love."

With gratitude ~
Linda

Contents

My name is Rachel Victoria Rafaneli. I'm a marine biologist living in Rhode Island in Southern New England; and this is the story of how one mischievous, miniature Dachshund changed everything in my world.

This is our magical story...

In the Beginning

My Aunt Rosalie wanted my parents to name me Rachele Rosalie Vittoria, but my mother said, "no, I think it will be just, "Rachel Victoria," "a little bit American with a beautiful Italian last name to make us proud."

I grew up in Johnston, Rhode Island just outside of Providence in a very large Italian family. I had so many aunts, uncles and cousins it was like an on-going celebration at our house where the kitchen was never empty.

It seemed as though my mother never stopped making coffee, and my father's home-made wine from his own small vineyard in the backyard kept the glasses filled and all his cronies happy!

I was the middle child with my brother Robert being the oldest by two years, and my sister Pasqualina (Patsy), younger by three years; and for the most part we all got along well. Maybe because there were so many people giving us equal notice, we never felt there was any need for competition for grown-up attention.

If we did get a little rowdy, all my father had to do was raise an eyebrow and we knew he meant business, prompting us to stop whatever we were doing in that moment. For the most part, our father was a mild-mannered man, but I had seen him push an obnoxious and somewhat threatening salesman over our Azalea bush one day, like he was swatting a fly! A temperament going back to the "old country" no doubt, where he grew up in a very tough province.

We knew the respect my dad had among the neighbors for being fair-minded, but also for his sense of humor and his animated way of telling his rambling stories about his birthplace in Italy and the shady characters he had known. I loved my father dearly and we learned respect for our parents at an early age. There was no talking back, or having a "smart mouth" as it was called in our house. We knew to be polite, or face the wrath of our father which would mean being sent to our room for the rest of the day and having no supper. Oh, and we did not have televisions in our rooms. It was like solitary confinement if we forgot our manners. So needless to say, we were pretty much on our best behavior…. most of the time.

Both my parents had a subtle way of making us laugh and shared a dry sense of humor that at times would send all of us, who were sitting around the dinner table, into hysterical laughter. I cherished those family moments and still do; and am so grateful for such a loving family.

We spent many hours with my dad at one of the ocean inlets along Narragansett Bay, called Galilee, where we dug for clams and quahogs. I would look forward to hearing him make his almost weekly announcement, "you kids get out your waders… we're going digging." I would grab my "clam" pants as I called them, and my raggedy sneakers, but knew I would be digging with my hands and bare feet by the end of the morning. My sister would always grumble about going; but she was the first at the table that night when our mother served up a big batch of steamers and stuffed quahogs, using an old family recipe with many spices along with onions, peppers and Italian sausage.

My brother Robert, absolutely hated going anywhere near the muddy ocean water, and we all knew when he was old enough to protest and make his own decisions, we would never see him at the ocean's edge again. That prophecy turned out to be completely accurate; because an adult with his own family, he built a pool in his backyard and that was the closest he ever got to water for swimming! I don't think he ever went down to the beautiful beaches in the summer. Guess he really had enough as a child!

I, however, only grew fonder of the crystal clear sea waters and the life hidden under the mysterious blue-gray waves, that at certain times of the day in the late spring, would turn into the most beautiful candescent teal color one could ever imagine. It was breathtaking, and I couldn't get enough of it. I wanted to learn everything there was to know about the creatures who lived in the ocean.

My room was like a mini-aquarium with several betta fish, two turtles, a gecko, and small crabs in painted shells. I once heard my mother say, "that girl would have a dolphin in there if she could." I *loved* dolphins!

A very special car trip to a real aquarium in Mystic, Connecticut was the highlight of my life (at that time), and I thought it was the most wonderful place I had ever seen. My father took me and two of my cousins who he thought would also enjoy the day. I was so excited I couldn't sleep the night before going, and the night after coming back too because I couldn't stop thinking about all the wonderful sea life I had seen, "up close and personal."

I would have lived there if I could have stayed! I especially loved the Beluga Whales because they swam right up to the glass to see me, and I just knew that *they* knew I loved them! To this day, I can't remember any other event that thrilled me as much as coming face to face with all the amazing ocean creatures I had only imagined and read about in books.

After going to Mystic I looked at food differently. I would analyze all cooked seafood on my plate and would spend more time dissecting clams and shrimp than eating them. "Just eat them, Rachel," my mother would say, "you don't have to know them personally!"

When I was about twelve, I had a screaming fit when I saw my mother start to toss a live lobster into the boiling pot just as she had done for years, but for some reason it now caused me great concern and stress. "No, no, stop!" "You can't kill them like that," I said. "Rachel, what is the matter with you?" said my father and sent me to my room. I ate nothing that night.

Since then, I have cooked many lobsters by the same method as my mother, but I now know that lobsters feel no pain because they lack the brain sensors to experience it. Now I enjoy eating lobsters as one of my most favorite foods. I do thank them though, for providing the wonderful meal I am about to enjoy… before sending them to their demise!

During that time, my parents thought I was becoming

obsessed with my passion for sea life, and I heard them discussing getting a pet for me. I liked that idea, and two days later we had a Beagle puppy. She immediately loved my dad exclusively, and barked incessantly. No matter what I did, "Betsy" (I named her that), would not come to me at all. My father would only have to look her way and she would run to him! He called her "stupido!" She responded to that name. I would stay in my room and talk to "Patrick," my gecko. He liked me better than Betsy did.

My obsession for the ocean stayed with me as I got older, and I began my marine-life studies in high school, college and then graduate school; and eventually a career in marine biology. It was my destiny, and I would always remain, *"the little fish girl,"* as my father called me,…forever.

Going Forward ~ My New Life Begins!

I had been living alone for some time as an adult in my own home in Providence, not too far from my parents. I had dinner there several times a week and stayed involved in my family's on-going everyday events. We were a very close family and I wanted it to continue, even if I moved to another town.

My graduate work was grueling and I was traveling back and forth from Providence to the University of Rhode Island in the southern part of the state for some of my classes, and then clinical studies at the Department of Fisheries. I also needed my scuba diving license, and there just didn't seem to be enough hours in the day with the sixty mile round trip.

In the winter it was worse with so much ice and snow, and it took me twice as long to get to my classes on time. Sometimes I just couldn't get there at all if the storm required drivers to stay off the highways, which happens often in New England until the plows can do their job. I really needed to make my life easier.

I decided in the spring to make changes that would take me out of the city!

But first, something extraordinary happened that seemed to be completely out of my control.... and here is what took place on that fateful day ---

DAY ONE - MYSTERIOUS MEETING

It started off as a very normal, bright and sunny Saturday morning. I had recently returned home from traveling for my new temporary job as a research analyst for the Marine and Fisheries Department at the University of Rhode Island; and today for some unknown reason I woke up thinking, "this is the first day of the rest of my life, and from here on in it is going to be even more excellent!"

It was one of those happy gut feelings that just washes over you every once in a while for no obvious reason, but you welcome it when it happens.

I had the top down on my convertible as I drove into the small shopping center in town to pick up a birthday card for a friend, and quite by accident instead of walking into the card shop as I had been doing for years, I strolled through the door next to it that happened to be a new pet shop. I was looking down at my cell phone and when I glanced up I was facing a large cage full of Dachshund puppies. I couldn't believe I went into the wrong store! It was not my nature to do something like that as I'm usually much more focused on what I'm doing.

It must be true what they say about cell phones, they **do** distract you. This was certainly proof of that!

As I was now **in** the store I looked around a bit. Being a Saturday, the shop was very crowded and the noise must have contributed to the puppies' excitement, because they were running and jumping as if they had swallowed Mexican jumping beans! All of them except **one**, who was standing perfectly still in the front corner of the large cage *... **looking at me***!

He wasn't moving, and for a moment I thought he was one of those furry toy puppies you see in a gift shop, but he moved his head just enough to let his eyes follow me as I walked past. "He **is** real," I thought, "and so cute!"

It was a little unsettling to be watched with such intensity, so I walked down to the end of the aisle and peeked around the corner to see if he had joined his rowdy brothers and sisters in play, but much to my surprise he was still looking my way. I walked back down to the cage and when I did he started wagging his long and pencil-thin tail acting as if he knew me. I was quite flattered that he picked me out of so many people. He really wanted me to notice him, and I certainly did! He was probably thinking, "mission accomplished."

This Dachshund pup was absolutely adorable, standing "tall" or should I say "short," and very proud and calm for such a little guy. He was only a few inches in height and had the shortest legs I had ever seen on a dog. He was tan and black and had a "mask" that was perfectly symmetrical that made him look quizzical and comical at the same time. He appeared to be smiling because his natural lip line under his very black nose was turned up a bit. He made me smile because he looked like **he** was smiling at **me**!

So we stood there smiling at each other until suddenly without giving it any further thought at all like I was hypnotized, I knew I must adopt this little guy and bring him home with me that same day! The birthday card I originally intended to purchase that morning, was not even a distant memory at that moment.

I felt as though we had known each other before I "mistakenly" arrived in the pet store and came face to face with this mysterious and tenacious "hot dog," as Dachshunds were called because of their shape. The mutual attraction was overwhelming. I kind of loved this little pup already. Could it be love at first sight for both of us? I was pretty sure the answer was "yes!"

I spoke with the store manager to work out the details of adoption, and then the black and tan pup was taken out of the large cage and placed in my arms belly-side up with his ears hanging back. A 10+ on the cuteness scale for sure!

My first thought was, "oh my gosh he is such an innocent little dog," especially with those big dark puppy eyes looking up at me with such intelligence and sweetness. I will always remember that special moment and how I felt. Maybe like a new mom leaving the hospital with her baby. Or, at least something similar. Christmas morning came to mind, remembering when I was a little girl waiting to see what Santa had left for me. That butterfly feeling in your stomach that was a combination of anticipation and excitement all rolled into one. I was ten years old again with a new puppy!

The pup gave a quick look back at the cage where

his brothers and sisters continued jumping around and chomping on each other's heads. One was actually pulling another one around by the tail, and they seemed to be completely oblivious to the fact that their brother was being taken away. One last look back and we left the store now heading for home, *together.*

Going Home

I placed the small animal carrier in the passenger seat, stretched the seat belt around it and put the top up on my car. I didn't want to cause my new friend any more stress than he must have been feeling already with being separated from his family and the warmth of the pet shop. I talked to him all the way home but he was completely silent. No whimpering or crying like little puppies do when they are nervous or anxious, and I was surprised by his bravery in accepting his abrupt transition.

At a stop sign, I looked into the carrier and he just looked right back as though he had done this many times, but I knew he hadn't. "Trusting" was the word that came to mind when I wondered how he could be so still.

In my wildest dreams that morning, I never thought I would be coming back home with a puppy; and I was of course, not prepared for the changes and adjustments that I would have to make now that I had a pet to take care of.

Before I left the shop I had purchased a soft round bed, a few toys, a harness with a leash, pads for the floor (until he was trained), dishes, food, and a large kennel cage as the store manager had suggested.

My house had a fenced in back yard so that was a plus,

and there was plenty of room to roam around. I lived alone but that was now changing, and I couldn't even begin to imagine how different my life would be when I let my very serious new friend out of his carrier, and he entered **my** world for the very first time.

At first he was very reluctant to walk around the house and he just sat down next to my feet. He was so small and I'm sure these new surroundings looked very large and scary to him. Humans must have appeared to be giants.

He whimpered just a little, so I picked him up and took him to sit on the couch with me and he snuggled up on my lap and instantly fell asleep. It never occurred to me that he must be exhausted. He was after all, just a baby. I dared not move because he looked so peaceful, and I must admit I was honored that he felt so secure with me. So what could I do? I took a nap too.

I had purchased everything I needed to make my new puppy comfortable in my home which was now his as well, and I made an appointment with a veterinarian for Monday to make sure "Mr. no name" was healthy. I had a document from the pet shop stating that he had his first puppy shots, but I wanted to have him set up with his very own doctor who would follow his health and well-being as he grew to be an adult Dachshund or "Doxie" as they were called, which I found out later.

Settling In

Puppy had so many toys that my family and friends gave him those first few weeks, that sometimes it was hard to find him in the midst of them. Some were bigger and longer than he was! He loved his kennel cage and dragged everything into it. I called it his "room." Sometimes if he had an accident and missed the pad, I would say, "c'mon puppy-face, go to your room now." After awhile he knew what I meant but he loved his room, so it was actually no big deal for him to go there. I didn't always take him outside because early spring in New England could be quite cold and sometimes the back steps would be a little too frosty for a bathroom trip down into the yard.

He loved his soft bed that was stuffed into the cage and he would often drag it out and around the house putting it where he wanted it. Usually next to where I was working on my computer. When I finished I would say, "time for dinner, let's get cooking!" I would walk towards the kitchen and he would walk along too, stumbling a bit but dragging his bed into the kitchen where he would get comfortable and watch me prepare dinner.

He had one very favorite toy that my little niece Lexi gave him the first time she came over to meet him. It was a squeaky rubber deer, but the endless squeaking when he played with it led me to remove the squeaker to maintain my sanity. He didn't seem to mind and carried the deer around with him everywhere by the antlers. Sometimes he would shake it wildly and send it flying across the room. Once it landed in my friend Jack's popcorn bowl and we had to re-pop a new batch! But we all laughed; and when the pup got the deer back, I think it had a little salt on it because he licked it for a couple of minutes before putting it away in his room, on top of his red plaid blanket. It was truly his favorite among an assortment of at least a dozen different doggie toys.

Puppy Names Himself

Several weeks had gone by and I still hadn't come up with a name that suited him. It absolutely had to be the right name! Being a fan of the New York Yankees baseball team, I thought of, *Bronx, Mickey, Jeter* and so on, but I was surrounded by Boston Red Sox fans so I just couldn't do it, but friends felt obligated to suggest every *other* possible name they could think of, from *Toby, Milton, Shamy, Snoopy, Ozzie,* and the list went on, but nothing sounded quite right.

One Sunday, my five-year old nephew Jayden was visiting and watching the children's channel while I was on the couch texting a friend, and "puppy-face," or "smarty pants," as I had started calling him, began barking. I jumped at the sound because he wasn't a dog who did a lot of barking. In fact, the first time he heard a noise outside that prompted him to bark, he surprised himself and looked at me as if to say, "where did that sound come from?" I said, "that was you, you silly dog." He tilted his head and raised his ears. "It was?"... he would have said if he could.

He had been watching television too with Jayden from half on and half off my lap, and apparently was fascinated with the little animated toy in the cartoon that was running back and forth in some sort of race with another neon colored character.

The little dog-like toy won the race and Jayden said, "yay, Oscar won!"

I asked him which one was Oscar and he described the one running back and forth that my pup got excited about.

"Hmm," I thought, "Oscar." That's an interesting name. Could that be it?

I looked at my pup who was now dozing off into puppy dreamland and said, "is that who you are... **Oscar?**" He opened his eyes just a bit and made a low murmuring sound I had not heard him make before and I also thought his smile turned up just a bit more, so I took that as a definite "yes!" **Oscar it was!** A name at last... thank heaven!

I looked up the name's meaning on my laptop and it was mythological for "lover of deer." Well that clinched it! He was a lover of deer because there was his favorite toy deer lying right beside him. One leg chewed completely off, but an object of love if I ever saw one.

And that was how Oscar named himself; and when I looked at him more closely, I could see that a was perfect name for him.

"Oscar," or "Mr Oscar" when I wanted to sound stern with him, or when he was mischievous, I would even call him "Mr. Oscar Pants," because he was such a "smarty pants." He answered to all *three* names.

The Floppy-Eared Burglar

Oscar became socialized at an early age because of practically everyone I knew coming in and out to frequently visit. Being from such a large family who all love dogs, Oscar became the darling of the family immediately.

He grew a bit taller and longer and became an adolescent young dog in no time. He was easy going, loved everybody and was a clown above all clowns. His best trick was kleptomania followed by his acting ability to look positively innocent of all charges. "Who me?" was always written all over his face!

Once, the repairman came in to fix the electrical box in the kitchen and left his tool belt on the floor. Every last plastic-handle tool and flashlight had gone missing, and with such swiftness it was like they just disappeared into thin air. The repairman followed me around looking for his missing tools, but I was fairly certain I knew where to find them… they would be in Oscar's "room." There was such a high bump under his blankets there was no way he could plead "not guilty" this time.

The repairman laughed as I crawled in to retrieve his tools and flashlight. It was a tight fit for me with so much stuff in there. My dog, the thief, did not keep a neat room.

Oscar looked on making a few low muttering sounds that I suspect were protests because I was removing his new-found treasures that he had taken to his favorite hiding place. The repairman thanked me and patted Oscar on the head saying, "sorry old buddy, I can't work without these," and Oscar looked longingly at the tools back in the belt where they belonged.

Oscar's room was the large dog cage that I bought at the pet shop the day I brought him home, but Oscar himself had decorated it with all of his favorite blankets, toys and anything else from around the house that struck his fancy. He had an innate ability to hide stolen objects under his blankets, push them into a heap and go to some other area of the house until the coast was clear. I often had one sock missing, and I always knew right where it was. Unfortunately by the time I would find it, it had holes chewed in it. Oscar just loved socks!

The Tiny Thief Has Sharp Teeth

I was happy to purchase a new cell phone that held lots of information that I could access quickly, so not only was it a phone, but I could keep work programs stored in it too. I called it my super-duper robot phone.

However, I made one big mistake with it. *I left it on the couch!*

It didn't take long for me to notice it was missing because it was in my hand constantly. I looked in between the couch cushions, under the couch, around on the floor, in my tote carrier, everywhere in the kitchen and then realized…"aha, Oscar the thief strikes again!" But, my phone? Is he making calls now?

Oscar was actually sitting in his room half covered with his red plaid blanket watching me when I walked over and said, "Oscar, do you have my new phone in there?" He wagged his curved tail which wagged the rest of his body. I crawled in, started pulling out blankets and toys and, "voila" there was my phone in the corner under a green dragon!

I would have found some humor in it except that the minute I picked it up and looked at it, I could see that one corner was completely chewed.

"Oh no, not my new phone!" "How could you get your teeth into this?"

If I could have read Oscar's mind, I think he was saying, "It was easy." "I just chewed and chewed and when the paint came off in my mouth, I just put it over in the corner with my dragon."

As luck would have it, the phone still worked just fine and so what if it looked a little mangled on one side. I should have known better than to leave such temptation right out in plain sight.

I was still learning, and Oscar was after all still a pup and curious about everything. How could I stay angry when he was just doing what dogs do....they chew on things; apparently **all** things!

Little Caped Crusader

Oscar really did love his blankets and dragged them around everywhere. He would roll around in the small soft blankets wherever he took them. If I was watching television, he would pull one up on the couch - (no small undertaking if I didn't help him), and lay on it while he watched television with me. He chewed holes in them and often would be dragging one around with his leg through a hole, amusing himself by playing with the blanket that was mysteriously following him. Sometimes, there was a huge tear, and he would get his head through it and walk around with the blanket around his neck trailing behind him. I called him the "caped crusader" because it didn't seem to bother him, and I think he actually liked wearing a blanket cape! All he needed was a crown for his head, and he could have been "King Oscar!" But as we all know, he already was King Oscar with or without a cape!

Oscar became so attached to his blankets that when it came time for laundry day and I threw them all in to be washed, he would get quite anxious and sit in front of the washing machine and then the dryer until they were finished. He barely took a break away until he heard the dryer buzzer go off and then pestered me until I took the blankets out. I never got to fold them because his jumping for joy at the sight of them coming out of the dryer, and wanting them all immediately while they were still warm, could not be delayed.

I would throw them into a heap on the floor and he would drag as many as he could either into his cage, or next to it. He would lay on them, or roll around in them like they were old friends who just returned home. Most had those large holes in them and they were, of course, his favorites.

The First Walk Outside on a Leash

The red harness leash was an adventure in itself to get it on Oscar, and he clearly didn't like it.

It was new to him and uncomfortable, so he twisted, jumped, growled at it, and resisted as much as he could; but because I was stronger and faster, I managed to get it on him. A few strong words were needed though and I had to say to him, "Mr. Oscar, stop jumping and squirming; we are going for a walk, you will love it, and that's that!"

He had no idea what I was saying, but off we went and once we got outside he was thrilled to be walking along with me, even with a few gentle tugs on the leash to keep him from running full speed ahead. So down to the river path we went.

Oscar's first glance at the river actually frightened him a bit and he didn't know how to react to the noisy rush of motion. Bewilderment and surprise were two of the emotions that played across his face, along with ear adjustments in constant motion to the new sounds of the moving water.

Straining a bit at his harness but not sure enough of himself to advance any further towards the fascinating but scary new sight, he held his ground. After a few minutes of sniffing around, digging up some dead leaves and taking in all the new sights, I said, "come on Oscar, time to go home." He was happy to continue our first walk together up on the sidewalk, and the next time I took out the harness and leash he was eager to have it put on and go for the next walk; and the many more walks to come after that.

Emergency Trip to the Vet's

One morning I was rushing around trying to get Oscar over to my parents, and then to campus on time for the last class on underwater mapping that I needed for my graduate studies. I had put my tote bag on one of the high stools at my kitchen counter.

Regrettably, in the time it took me to run upstairs to grab my laptop, Oscar, tempted by the hanging cloth straps, pulled it onto the floor and emptied it of most of its contents; non of which was of much interest to him with the exception of the plastic *aspirin* bottle.

By the time I got back down the stairs, he had skillfully managed to eat through the bottle. Plastic was no challenge for his sharp puppy teeth and the aspirin tablets were scattered all over the floor. I was horrified and riveted at the same time as to what he was doing, and I knew he had eaten some because he was making a very strange face with his tongue licking in and out, obviously because of the bitter taste of the aspirin.

I never in my life moved as quickly as I did in that moment to get him into his carrier, calling my vet at the same time and rushing out the door to put the carrier holding Oscar, into the back of my car. Oscar seemed surprised that we were moving so quickly to go for a "drive!" He had no idea that he had eaten something that could potentially make him **very** sick.

Calling ahead prepared the staff to have everything ready because of possible kidney and liver damage. They were completely set up for Oscar and rushed him in immediately. Blood work was done, charcoal was given, lots of fluids and an overnight stay as a precaution to monitor him, was necessary. Oscar was very compliant and loved all the attention. Actually, I think he enjoyed the whole ordeal. Well, maybe not the charcoal.

I was a complete wreck throughout the crisis and terribly guilt ridden but Oscar was fine and no harm was done. Owning a pet is a big responsibility; a fact that I became very well aware of that day, and one I have remained constantly aware of. I was *never* that careless again.

A Temporary New Home
for Me and Oscar

As I was going to be re-locating to the southern part of
Rhode Island where I worked and was still taking classes
at the university, Oscar and I temporarily moved in with
my mom and dad until my new place in Narragansett was
ready. I had rented out my house in Providence more
quickly than I had anticipated, so we needed an in-between
place to live for a short period of time.

My parents were thrilled to have me back at least
for a little while, and prepared my old room like I had
never left. Oscar had visited many times and the attention
he received was beyond description. He was, after all,
Oscar... the king of all dogs!

Mom and dad should have a revolving door in their
home because aunts, uncles cousins, and neighbors come
and go on a regular basis. It's just the way it is in Italian
families.

Long talks ensue at the kitchen table and there is
endless food and drink for everyone.. Oscar thought he
was in heaven.

Constant attention with pats on the head, rough-housing

with my dad, many available laps to curl up on and little surprise bits of food the likes of which he had never tasted before; but much to my horror caused him all kinds of tummy distress that somehow only became known when he was sitting on **my** lap…phew!

Staying at my parents' home had been like one long party for Oscar. New toys arriving almost daily, and *soooo* much attention. I said, "you know, Oscar, in a few more weeks we are moving to our new house near the ocean and it will be just you and me again." He looked at me with that unwavering smile as if to say, "that's just fine with me!"

During that stay at my parents, Oscar became totally trained to let me know when he had to go outside. He would whine and pace near the door and I would take him out into the back yard. Most of the time he would make it only as far as the back step welcome mat and it became his favorite *spot*. My dad said, "well, it does say *welcome!*"

Some days I was able to encourage him to go further out into the yard but the winds can be very gusty in Rhode Island and several times when he was trying to squat (he never lifted his leg), the wind would come up and blow him over.

He would lie on the ground for a minute staring across the yard at me, as if to say, "do you see what's happening here?" But eventually he would accomplish his task and run back up on the porch eager to return to the warmth of the wood-burning stove in the kitchen.

Oscar had a strange habit of once coming back into the house, running full speed through the downstairs rooms, sliding across the kitchen floor and just zooming around as fast as his little legs could run until he was completely worn out.

Then he would go into his room, crawl under a blanket and rest. My dad commented that he had never seen such a display of happiness and relief just because he had gone out to the bathroom.

He said to my mother, "suppose **I** ran all around the house like that when I came out of the bathroom?" My mother with a completely straight face said "yes, and then I would drive you **directly** to the mental facility."

I laughed at the thought of my rather robust father running full speed around the house like my little Oscar!

Before we moved to our new home, I made an appointment for Oscar to visit Miss Karen, his veterinarian, for two needed surgeries. Her practice wasn't that far from where we were staying with my parents, and I wanted to get it over with before the hassle of moving was upon us.

Visiting the Vet for Two Needed Surgeries

Before Oscar could be neutered he had to reach five pounds and when that day came he joyfully hopped into the car not knowing his fate.

If he only knew what was in store for him he might just have run the other way; instead of stampeding directly into the vet's office and around the back of the front counter where the staff was waiting for him, and greeted him like the Kind of England, or at least the Prince of Wales. If he only knew because of his teeth crowding, he would be returning home the next day with two less teeth, and two less other body parts as well.

He, however, was non the wiser and as usual just loved all the attention; but he did whimper a bit when I picked him up to go home, from the tenderness of his surgery, so I was very gentle with him for a few days. "C'mon my big boy now with straight teeth….let's go home." He barked once rather quietly, and I thought his voice sounded a bit deeper than usual. *Must have been my imagination.*

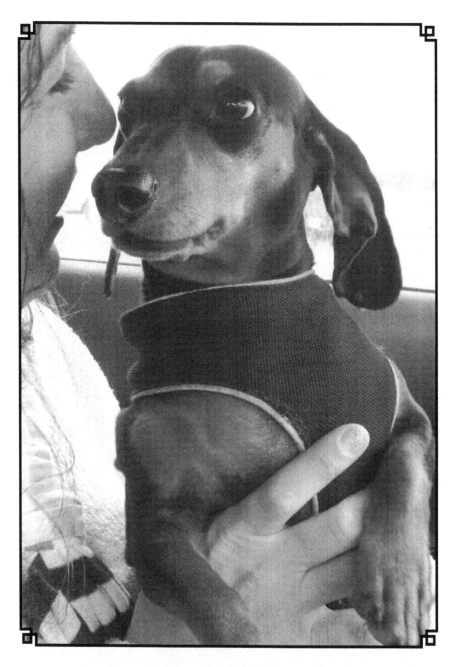

Oscar Shares a Smile

Silent Intruder

A week or so before we were moving, I was packing some things for our new place. It was very early in the morning and I had let Oscar outside and then back in but I realized I hadn't seen him for awhile. I didn't want to wake up mom and dad, so I went around the house whispering, "Oscar, where are you?" Again...."Oscar come out, where in the world are you?" Then I heard through the small opening in my parents' room, my fathering saying in a low gruff voice, **"he's in here!"**

When I opened the door and looked in I couldn't believe my eyes. There was my mom sound asleep on one side of the bed, my dad on the other trying to look angry, and my little Oscar right in the middle all snuggled in and sharing a pillow on my dad's side. Apparently he had crawled his way up under the blankets until he found just the right spot in between two of his favorite people. I started laughing quietly but my dad got up holding Oscar dangling at arms length saying, **"he is not allowed in our bed! Your mother and I do have our limits!"**

I continued to smile but I knew how much they would both miss him when we moved and that my dad was an old softy when it came to Oscar.

I hoped they would drive down to our new place to visit, but the typical Rhode Islander, especially the older generation, doesn't like to drive too far from where they live. It's just a quirky Rhode Island thing.

Slight Delay

Before moving I had to spend three days at the Cape Cod Research Center in Buzzards Bay, Massachusetts. It was a two hour drive and it wasn't practical to drive back and forth. It was part of my studies to research eco-systems and possibly do further work at the Chesapeake Bay Environmental Center in Maryland, but that was not determined yet. My parents would take care of Oscar until I returned, but due to a freak accident I came back home sooner than anticipated.

My first day in the water an angry Blue Crab, who probably didn't want this strange intruder in his living room, got me in his pincers and dug deep into my ankle giving me a nasty wound. Because of the possibility of infection I returned home until there was no sign of a problem. I am always up-to-date with my shots so I wasn't all that worried. My trip to Maryland was postponed and our moving day was in sight, so we had many things to get done.

Oscar was not one to hide his emotions, and when he saw me coming through the kitchen door, he began Olympic high-jumps into the air and making his happy barking sounds that could be heard two streets away.

I got down on the floor to help calm him, but to no avail. I was stomped upon, hit in the face with his whip-like tail moving at warp speed; and generally trampled until I picked him up and held him tight. Thank heaven he wasn't a Great Dane! What can I say? He missed me! And I certainly missed him too!

Moving to the Coast

When we moved into our new place just a short walk from the beaches along Narragansett Bay, it was like landing on another planet for Oscar. Everything was so open and new to him. Not at all like being in the city.

I had lived in and around Providence for most of my adult life and I never minded the forty-five minute drive to South County where the beaches stretched along the coastline, and now I was living there and working at home. It was just wonderful, and a dream come true.

Sometimes at night we could look out across the bay and see the white light from the Beavertail Lighthouse in Jamestown that rotates counter clockwise every seven seconds. On foggy nights we could hear its foghorn blasts and Oscar would always cock his head trying to figure out what that strange noise was. I, myself, loved the sound of it. It was eerily calming and my mind would drift to the sailing vessels in the heavy fog heeding its warning, that the rocky coastline was near.

I had two more classes to complete my advanced master's program, an MS in Marine Biological Sciences and I would be a certified Marine Biologist. This was my eighth year of school and I had begun in the Provincial Fish and Wildlife Branch after receiving my bachelor's degree. I was especially interested in the study of the evolution and diversity of ocean fishes courses, and wanted to pursue something in that field when I graduated.

I still had to be re-certified in scuba diving but that was no problem living in this area. I had worked hard for many years and everything was finally falling into place; and Oscar and I were living in one of the most beautiful seacoast regions on the East Coast to be involved in this type of work. The natural resources were incredibly abundant here in Rhode Island. Such a beautiful state!

Rachel and Oscar exploring

Oscar Meets the Ocean

When Oscar saw the Atlantic Ocean for the first time, it reminded me a little of the river incident when he was younger and more easily frightened with new and strange places. But now in his grown-up dog fearlessness, he was just plain mesmerized and awestruck with the soft sand, interesting objects like sea shells, seaweed, and stones of every size. You see... Oscar just loved stones.

He seemed genuinely captivated with everything around him, but when the gentle waves washing in with the tide on this early spring day caught his attention, he jumped back a bit even from this considerable distance. He made a quick sharp growly noise never having seen the ocean before and ran a few haltering feet toward the shore; but then at my urging followed me more confidently down to the water's edge where the sand was wet. He looked puzzled by the feel of it and pranced a little not knowing how to balance himself on the wet squishy sand. He looked like he was performing in a dog show, walking like one of those high steppers trying to impress the judges!

But it didn't take him very long to adapt to the new surroundings, because after a few more minutes of exploration and challenging the incoming surf, you'd think he had lived his whole life on the beach. He loved it! I could always tell when Oscar loved something because he would bounce up and down with excitement. Now it was like he had "springs" in those little legs! Bouncing and running along at the same time with both ears folded back in the wind!

(I must say, that sometimes, my adorable Dachshund was just a little peculiar looking!!)

Then he began digging furiously in the sand, perhaps the way his ancestors had done hundreds of years before in Germany, when the hunters sent out Dachshunds to dig for badgers. The name of the breed "Dachshund" comes from two German words: "dachs" meaning badger, and "hund" meaning dog, and also… "one who hunts below ground."

Oscar would stop and run with me along the water's edge sniffing and feeling the coldness of the ocean, this time of the year being around 50 degrees. I myself did not want to get my feet wet for at least another two months. New England weather was not always that comfortable in April.

Oscar would pick up a stone every now and then and quickly spit it out tasting sand and salt for the first time. Seaweed was a challenge for him and I doubled over laughing as I watched him crawl under a mound of it like he does with his blankets, but he got quite tangled in the cold wet weeds. He growled at it, ran around in circles with it hanging off his head, tripping a couple of times and finally freeing himself when his back legs pulled it off while he was running. "Go Oscar", I yelled, "you get that bad seaweed!"

Harbor Seals at Point Judith

I became quite familiar with the winter Harbor Seals while doing research on the cold-weather visitors, and I would often call Oscar my little Harbor Seal because they looked somewhat alike with their black noses and constant vocalization when excited.

The seals also will eat rocks but unfortunately because silly humans are getting too close to them while they are resting on the offshore sandbars, they get nervous and will actually swallow the rocks which is a very unhealthy thing for the agitated seals to do.

There is a law in Rhode Island that requires people to stay quite a distance away from the seals so as not to upset them, but unfortunately most people are just curious about them and don't realize their close proximity upsets the easily stressed mammals.

It always surprises me that some people don't know that you should never feed people food to any wildlife. Snacks they find in their cars like potato chips, candy, leftover sandwiches, orange peels or even clam cakes common to the beach area can often kill or make wildlife very sick.

Oscar and the Seagulls

Seagulls, however, may be the exception to this and I call them the scavengers and dumpster divers of the coastline. They will truly eat just about anything, and if you are at the beach enjoying the deep blue sky, beautiful ocean and clean fresh air, just don't hold that french fry or sandwich too far out because in one feld swoop a hungry gull will grab it and be out over the ocean before you can say, "hey what was that;? and, "where is my lunch?"

Seagulls are not fussy, and will really eat whatever you are holding or is on the blanket next to you. They will even fly down and steal hamburgers right off the grill while you are cooking them. Very aggressive and daring these always hungry gulls.

Oscar was barking more now that he was older and seagulls would especially send him into an uncontrollable need to keep up with their squawking. Sometimes I thought they were actually carrying on a conversation from the place where we were sitting on the sand, to the fence posts where they were perched.

"Squawk, bark," "squawk, squawk, bark, bark." I wondered what they were saying to each other.

Maybe: *"Got food?"* *"No."* *"Want to get some?"* *"Okay."* *"We will wait little dog, hurry up."*... And so on.

Oscar and I Go Exploring

Oscar and I frequently walked the shoreline nearby to where our house was situated on the bay, but several friends who lived about six miles south of us in Westerly wanted us to enjoy that part of the state as well, so we learned about Watch Hill, Misquamicut, Nappa Tree Point, and Weekapaug on the coast, and Wilcox Park up in town.

The area got congested when the tourists rolled into town in May, but it just added to the New England flavor of the area.

Rachel and Oscar looking out to sea

Oscar Finds Socks Everywhere He Goes

For our first visit we were going meet Chuck and Paula after a walk in Westerly's Wilcox Park. This beautiful and historic fifteen-acre recreational area is located in the middle of town. Paula said that in the spring and summer the park plays host to art fairs, concerts, and plays. There are fountains, monuments and beautifully maintained walking paths and a variety of small animals such as chipmunks, rabbits, and squirrels who call the park their home.

The paved walking paths in the park are wonderful for leashed dogs, and also for children who love to play on the grounds, or just sit on the large bronze statue of "The Runaway Bunny," from the book by Margaret Wise.

I was very anxious to check it out myself and take Oscar for his first walk in a "real" park.

Paula owned an antique book store on the main street in town called "The Greatest Lion," and Chuck had managed a large family-owned landscaping business for several years. They were dear friends and now I would have the opportunity to see them more often and introduce them to Oscar. They were dog people, too. They had a huge yellow Lab, "Lennon," named after John Lennon, their favorite Beatle.

So we went to the park, and Oscar was walking along quite proudly this bright and sunny day just enjoying the new views from his low range of vision. Suddenly, we came upon a very small white sock apparently dropped by the little boy in the stroller, quite a ways ahead of us. Before I knew it, Oscar picked up the little sock and started walking happily with it dangling from his mouth like it was supposed to be there - the sock swinging from side to side.

Up ahead on the path, we saw the woman with the stroller headed back and we knew she was looking for her little boy's sock. Sure enough, when we all got closer she burst out laughing at the sight of this tiny Dachshund walking along with the sock and said to her little boy, "look Zachary, that doggie has your sock!" She and "Zachary" met us and I said, "my dog Oscar and I were returning your sock and are glad you turned around and came back." "We weren't sure we could catch up to you." Oscar reluctantly released the sock and it was just as good as new. Mom thanked Oscar and the little boy got to pat Oscar on the head and off everyone went to continue their walks. Zachary with both socks on his little feet and Oscar now, sadly, sockless.

Oscar's Meltdown in the Park

We walked around the large pond at the far end of the park where Mallard ducks were swimming among the pond lilies. I thought Oscar might be interested in the ducks but he seemed a bit bored by them. I think they were too slow moving for him, but when a rather large squirrel ran across our path he became the incredible hulk-dog and I could hardly hold onto the leash!!!

I've never heard or seen such a commotion from him before. He went from quietly walking along as a small calm dog to an hysterical bouncing, jumping maniac the likes of which I had never seen before!

WHO WAS THIS TINY CRAZY DOG??????

Oscar was fairly reserved for a Dachshund, but not now! This giant squirrel- thing brought out the beast in him. Frantic barking, straining at his leash, jumping non-stop into the air, twirling around and getting twisted in his lead; yelping and whining all at the same time! I had never seen anything like it. OSCAR WAS POSSESSED!

I'm sure if the squirrel was now watching from a tree, he must have been belly laughing at the hysteria he had caused just by running across our path. Such power to make a little dog go completely senseless like that. Maybe the squirrel told the story to all his squirrel friends later, and they all had a good laugh about the little "hot dog" who went bonkers!

I finally had to pick up Mr. crazy-dog and walk away as quickly as possible before he fainted from the pure stress of not being able to run after the squirrel in some direction, any direction! I don't think it mattered to him.

It took me about ten minutes to calm him down and I prayed another squirrel didn't venture out anywhere near us. Or a chipmunk, rabbit or even a mouse! Who knew what reaction they might cause, and I didn't want to find out!

By the time we got over to Paula and Chuck's I was warn out, but Oscar was leaping around full of pep to be meeting new people and he and Lennon the lab, hit it off famously and romped around the back yard for the entire visit.

I told the story of the squirrel encounter, and found out that some of the squirrels in the park have been known to go after a dog, and actually bite them. Who knew? …..maybe Oscar did!

Driving home that day, I turned to look at my cutie pie in the back seat carrier and he was sound asleep. What a day! New friends to play with, meeting different people, and coming face to face with very scary "wild" animals in the park! A very full day indeed, in the life of Oscar.

Another Robbery and Hiding the Evidence

It wasn't all that long after the stolen and chewed phone incident, but I apparently hadn't learned my lesson. My designer sunglasses were on top of my head or on my face most of the time, but they were not in either place when I reached for them.

We had just come in from the back yard, and I looked down at Oscar who had been outside with me and watching me rake up some dead leaves to spruce up the yard for summer. Oscar turned his head up and wagged his tail …just because I looked at him. Such love. I adored him even though in the back of my mind I was thinking, "did you take my glasses, you little munchkin?"

I left Oscar inside the house and went back out to look for them.

I remembered putting them on the bench in the corner of the yard while I was picking up the leaves. I approached the bench, but **no** glasses. "Could Oscar have taken my sunglasses?"

But how could he have taken them without me seeing him and what would he have done with them? There is no kennel out there and no blankets to hide them in. So I went back into the house and let him outside and said, "Oscar, did you take my glasses?" He jut sat there looking up at me. I raised my voice and said, "Mr. Oscar Pants, you go and find my glasses right now because I know you took them." **"Go get my glasses!"**

I started running around the yard looking here and there and he just got excited and began barking at the game I was playing, but amazingly enough he ran in back of the large Lilac bush near some rocks and came out proudly carrying my glasses by the side piece.

"Oscar, give me those glasses!" He ran the other way with them and the chase was on. I caught up rather quickly because a long-distance runner he was not. By the time I got the glasses out of his mouth they were a completely chewed mess. I wondered when he had the time to chew them so evenly all around. Even the lenses were mangled beyond repair. "Oscar, look what you did to my beautiful sunglasses," I said. He looked at them and then barked, probably because he wanted to go and hide them again, but this game was over and I had no sunglasses. But, I really did learn my lesson **this** time.

Don't leave anything lying around, Rachel!

What A Surprise!

My friends Lucy and David from school, were married last year and I was Lucy's maid of honor. We were close friends and when they bought a summer cottage at Misquamicut Beach just a few miles south of Narragansett, they invited me and anyone I wanted to bring with me, over for a cookout to celebrate the Fourth of July. Of course Oscar went just about everywhere with me and I was taking care of my little niece Lexi that day, so she happily came along too.

Oscar was wearing his finest red, white and blue neckerchief, and Lexi and I were dressed comfortably for the 95 degree day. Usually it is cooler near the water, but this particular day even the ocean breeze couldn't cool it off. The seagulls were unusually sedated by the heat too and more quiet than usual.

The television weather people called this a "three **H** day"… hazy, hot and humid! It was my kind of weather and perfect for the beach.

I hadn't seen Lucy and David for a few months, and it was a nice reunion to join them for this holiday celebration with family and friends. When Lucy said, "I have a surprise for you guys," and went back inside from the deck on the back of the house overlooking the ocean, I couldn't imagine what she meant, but when she came back out with a very diminutive puppy in her arms and said, "I want you all to meet Lucinda," I was completely captivated. She was a miniature long-hair *red* Dachshund just eight weeks old, and so small and sweet.

Baby Lucinda

"Look at the baby," I said to Oscar. He sniffed a bit but was really more interested in Lexi's ice cream cone than Lucinda.

It turned out to be a wonderful day at the beach. David

cooked burgers and hot dogs for the kids and had a huge pot of lobsters, sweet corn and steamers for the seafood loving adults. Lucy carved out a watermelon and filled it with every seasonal fruit you could imagine. And, of course there were fireworks all up and down the beach as soon as it got dark.

Oscar barked and barked but wasn't frightened at all like some dogs are when fireworks go off. Not my brave Oscar! I think he actually enjoyed them, and looked up into the display as the dazzling colorful lights lit up the night sky over the ocean. Lucy kept Lucinda in the house not wanting to frighten her by the loud booming of the fireworks out on the beach.

We left Misquamicut around ten and headed home. Oscar once again fell asleep in his carrier as did little Lexi in her car seat next to him. Two little sweethearts at the end of a fun summer day.

Getting to Know Lucinda

Whenever I had the time, I would pack up Oscar and head down to the beach to meet up with Lucy, who often took Lucinda out somewhere near the cottage for a walk. Lucinda, being a long-hair Doxie looked nothing like Oscar. She resembled a tiny Irish Setter with long red fur; and as she grew, her nose got more pointed. She was the complete opposite of Oscar who was "all boy," and she was just so dainty and feminine, especially with the ruffles and bows that Lucy loved dressing her in.

She wasn't interested in jumping around like Oscar did when he was trying to impress her. She was also not interested when he would stretch out in front of her in the "let's play" position. Lucinda was just hot having any of that foolishness! Oscar would often try barking directly into her face, quite rudely I thought, but nothing created any interest in her to oblige him in playing any ridiculous games. She was so blasé and almost stuck-up and I loved my silly little playful guy even more.

Lucinda's stand-offishness always puzzled Oscar. He just wanted a friend who would play with him. Was that asking too much? The more relentless he was, the more she would growl and I was concerned that Miss Sweetness and Light would eat my Oscar for lunch if he wasn't careful.

Lucinda Posing

Lucy was so patient and always tried to reason with Lucinda, but it was just her disposition. "Disagreeable" I called it, but I would never say so to Lucy. She adored her little fluffy red Dachshund with the dreadful personality.

As Lucinda grew out of her puppy awkwardness into adolescence, she became even more unpleasant. A "brat" some might say.

Lucinda was definitely not the kind of dog that would be a good match with children. That's why it is important to determine that before adopting a dog who would be raised with small children. You just have to be careful. Not all dogs are created equal in their personalities and temperament.

Oscar did not have a feisty side and I knew he would never snip or bite anyone under normal conditions. Lucinda was nick-named "devil-dog" by David, Lucy's husband, because one day she ran into the house from the beach while he was standing in the kitchen minding his own business, and bit him right on his big toe. Lucy said she couldn't help but laugh at David's hopping around the kitchen holding his toe, but David said it was quite painful because Lucinda has sharp little teeth!

There was also another time when Lucinda was out on the beach and stole a ball away from a little boy who was just playing and minding his own business. When he tried to get it back she chased him half-way down the beach growling, snarling and barking and brought the ball back home with her. I definitely agreed with David that Lucinda was for sure.. a red-haired "devil-dog" with bows!

Lucinda Napping

Attack at the Beach Market

The Breachway Convenience Mart on Atlantic Avenue was **the** place to go for anything you needed for the beach or picnics. Snacks, ice cream, a cup of coffee, sandwiches, or in our case a watermelon for dessert later at Lucy's. Kristina was the manager at the market and made the best deli sandwiches on Atlantic Avenue. All the beach people stopped in on a regular basis as did we because David loved the foot-long grinders with the special sauces that only Kristina knew how to make.

The mart was across from one of the private beaches so you could go in shoeless wearing your bathing suit, and even dogs were welcomed as long as they were leashed.

I went in first with Oscar followed by Lucy with Lucinda who was wearing bright purple ribbons on her head. Now that she was older, Lucy gave her bigger bows to wear.

There were two boys leaning their surfboards against the outside wall, and a few teenaged girls trying to decide which flavor of ice cream they were going to have.

When the girls saw Lucinda it was all "oohs and ahs," but they couldn't leave the line where they were standing. "Lucky for them," I thought. But just then one of the surfer boys, Lucy knew as "Evan," walked over to the dogs and before we were able to move out of their way, Lucinda lunged at the boy's ankle and bit it!

We were horrified, but saw right away as the boy jumped back that no harm had been done, except frightening all of us; especially the boy who was yelling some very unkind words at Lucinda who was now barking furiously at him for someone unknown reason, acting as if **she** were the victim.

After apologies were extended we left the store immediately forgetting about the watermelon, and Lucy said, "that's it! - Lucinda begins obedience school next week!" I noticed Oscar's smile turned up a bit.

After those incidences, I considered even more that she might just bite Oscar if he insisted on trying to get her to play with him. I would look at Lucinda and think, "how could such a fluffy little red dog with mops for paws be so ferocious and unsociable?" Again, it made me love my Oscar even more.

The Noodle Encounter

One night I was preparing a seafood dinner consisting of shrimp, scallops, mussels, and mushrooms over linguini, for a few friends from school who were coming over for dinner. We were having clam chowder first, and my kitchen was filled with the amazing smells of the abundant and mouth-watering foods from the sea. My next-door neighbors were having an in-ground clam bake with fresh lobsters; and the salty aromas from their seafood bake in the ground that was simmering under seaweed, were mingling with my kitchen scents reminding me once again of how much I loved New England and all the unique delicacies we could enjoy every day.

As I was finishing the noodles, Oscar was watching the steam rise in the air from the colander where they were cooling. My mischievous side took over and I pulled one of the long pasta pieces out and dropped it on the floor at his feet. Oscar, having never seen anything like this before, looked at it and then up at me as if to say, "what am I supposed to do with this long slimy wet thing?" Then he barked at it, but being a noodle it didn't respond.

So I picked it up and let it touch his nose and then very

gently wrapped it *around* his nose. He stood remarkably still while I played my silly game.

But then….he suddenly realized it **was** a game and got a little silly! Taking after his owner, no doubt. He shook his head violently while barking and jumping around in a circle sending the noodle flying, as it broke into pieces sticking to the chair, the floor, and my leg! Oscar didn't know quite what to do at that moment so he pounced on the piece on the floor and attacked it with great ferocity. My company was just coming in, so the noodle game sadly had to end with my picking up the pieces and Oscar looking very disappointed; but I assured him we would play this game again the next time I cooked pasta. He smiled at hearing the good news!

The Language of Oscar

Oscar didn't bark very much when he was a little pup, but as he grew his "speaking his mind" became more frequent. Not only did he bark at just about anything that moved, but any sound he didn't recognize. Any outside noise that threatened his territory initiated a response from him. He also had special sounds to express his emotions. One I call, "having the last word." I would say something like, "Oscar stop jumping up and down," and he would make a two syllable sound to finalize the conversation. It was a low whiney half growl and half grunt followed by lowering his head and pouting. I'm pretty sure he was saying, "I don't want to, but okay."

If I said, "do you want to go for a walk?" That question would set off instant hysteria and high pitched barking and whimpering sounds, that could probably be heard by dolphins and whales far out to sea. That meant, "Yippee! Let's go!, Let's go!, Let's go!" …..many times.

He also had a "catch me if you can" group of sounds that he would make if I said something like, "give me that squeaky toy," or "let me have that nice blankie," and he would respond with a low long growl followed by several short barks and a playful gurgling sound like he was gargling with mouthwash, --and then the chase was on for me to catch him with whatever he had in his mouth. He was pretty fast for a short kid.

Close Encounter at the Beach

Rhode Island beaches are known for their natural beauty, and tourists fill the sandy coastline every year from Memorial Day through Labor Day.

If you own a cottage on the beach it is like having a piece of heaven to have twenty-four hour access to such splendor. Summer nights looking out over the ocean with a star-lit sky can be breathtaking.

Lucy and David looked forward to their summers in Westerly and we all loved visiting with them and appreciated their sharing such a beautiful spot with us. My birthday is in August and unbeknownst to me, my sister Patsy and Lucy had planned a surprise party with about two dozen friends and family invited. It was a Sunday and in the high 90's so heading for the beach to visit friends was something to look forward to, and Oscar and I were on our way.

We loved to swim if the tide was in, but Oscar didn't like the feeling of the undertow when the waves went out and the sand dropped down under his feet. How could you blame him, being that small?

What we didn't know as we were driving down, was that Lucy and Lucinda had waded out into the water to join some neighbors to cool off. The lifeguard on duty that afternoon was being very watchful, because she had just received a message that there was a riptide along the beach line and to make sure no bathers were too far out. Riptides can be as close to shore as twenty-five feet, and there is often no warning until you feel the water pulling you sideways.

By the time Lucy and Lucinda felt the pull, it was too late. Lucy knew from experience to go along with it, and not fight against the water because it could carry you along further away from the shore.

Lucy waved to the lifeguard who knew immediately they were having a bit of trouble, and she quickly went out first to the woman holding the little dog. The others made it in okay further down the beach by swimming parallel to the shore until they were out of reach of the current. The lifeguard pulled Lucy and Lucinda onto the beach and everyone was fine, but it was a scary feeling to be pushed along by the strong side-ways rush of water.

When Oscar and I arrived they were just coming up the stairs into the house, and everyone was talking at once about what had happened. David was holding Lucinda who was hardly recognizable wrapped up in a towel. She had taken a dousing in the water, and looked like red seaweed. She was fine as was Lucy, but when David put Lucinda down and she started shaking off the water and sand, Oscar actually jumped back and growled. He didn't recognize his usually perfectly groomed Lucinda. She was a frightening sight!

All Ends Well with a Great Party

When I saw Aaron, Paula, Chuck, Penney, Diane and other friends and family I knew it was a surprise birthday party; and we soon put the mishap behind us and just had a great time.

Lucinda came out later to join the festivities after she was bathed and combed. She looked non-the-worse for the incident in the water, but when Aaron made the mistake of trying to pet her, Lucinda had to be banished into the house for the rest of the night for trying to bite him.

Aaron, luckily had quick reflexes, and pulled his hand away just in time. "That was a close call," Penney said to Aaron. "You almost lost a few fingers!" Aaron raised his eyebrows and said, "I won't be getting too close to that little dog again!"

My First Year with Oscar Comes to an End

As the end of our first year together was approaching and we were heading to Providence for Sunday dinner, my mom called and said, "wasn't it about a year ago that you adopted Oscar?" I told her he was 14 months old now and had been with me for a year. She said "I'll have to make some of those spicy meatballs and pasta for you both." I said, "absolutely not!" remembering the last time he had eaten spicy food in my mom's kitchen and how it upset his puppy tummy. But sure enough, Oscar was presented with a small bowl of meatballs that were cooked lean beef and bread crumbs, but **no** spices that mom had made special just for him. He devoured them so quickly you'd think he had never eaten before. But I guess compared to his regular dog chow, the meatballs must have tasted, well... very tasty!

Oscar Becomes a Retreiver

Oscar was becoming a mature Doxie and was much less of a thief and more of a retriever, as he would now find special things that he liked and bring them to me first before chewing them to pieces and hiding them, like he did when he was younger. Some of his new findings were the cordless mouse for my computer, my styling brush, my lipstick, and my sterling silver bracelet that had individual beads and charms representing various birthdays and special occasions. It was one of my most favorite things.

When I saw Oscar walking towards me with it hanging out of his mouth, I couldn't quite figure out at first what it was until he got closer. Apparently the safety chain had become lodged between his teeth and he was bringing it to show me.

"Oh for heaven sake, Oscar!" I said. "How did you manage to get my bracelet stuck in your teeth?" He sneezed and stuck out his tongue a couple of times, probably because the metal tasted bitter in his mouth. I pulled it out quite easily and said, "no more jewelry for you!" He stuck out his tongue again. Then he smiled.

Summer Breezes Take on a Chill

As the summer was winding down, and Labor Day was fast approaching as the signal for the tourists along the coast to pack up their campers and close up their cottages, Oscar and I said "good bye" to many friends. Lucinda was enrolled in a special anger-management class for dogs in Warwick where Lucy and David lived in the winter, to begin immediately when they got her back home. I could only hope she didn't flunk the course!

I must say though, that Oscar did eventually win her over with his patience, and she actually seemed to like him better by the end of the summer. She would even play with him on occasion, if she was in the right mood. Maybe there was hope for Lucinda after all!

Lucinda and Oscar.

We visited Wilcox Park again after a leisurely lunch with Chuck and Paula, and it was incident free. No squirrels this time, but Oscar was definitely on the alert looking this way and that. Lennon and Oscar once again played non-stop with a tennis ball in the back yard. We knew we wouldn't be heading down this way as often once the weather changed. Rhode Island life in the winter slows down a great deal as people just don't drive around as often as they do in the beautiful warmer months. It's just the way of Rhode Islanders.

I had begun to wonder what our first winter would be like living on the Bay with the snow, ice and frigid temperatures along the waterfront. It was of little concern to me though as I thoroughly enjoyed all the seasons in New England. I always looked forward to the next, wondering what that one would bring and never was weather boring along the Eastern Seaboard.

Driving could be difficult sometimes until the roads were plowed, but I had a four-wheel drive vehicle and I knew once the plows and sanders had come through all you had to do was slow down and drive safely. But as I was soon to learn, Oscar and I would not be in Narragansett **this** winter.

"Allie" Finds a New Home

Sunday night my dear friend Diane called from Wickford, where she lives with her tortoise breed female cat, "K.C." (a.k.a. Kitty Cat), in a beautiful old Victorian house right in the center of the village. She said she had some very exciting news, and that she had adopted a Dachshund from the local animal shelter, that she couldn't wait to tell me about.

Diane was always active with the animal rescue league helping out with fundraisers and printing out the annual newsletter to get the word out that many beautiful but desperate animals were just waiting to be adopted; and much to her delight a one-year old brindle-colored female Dachshund had come in after the owner had been in an unfortunate accident, and could no longer take care of her.

There was no hesitation for Diane. She brought the dog home that same day. She knew "K.C." would happily accept a new friend because she was a gentle cat with a sweet disposition.

Di was very anxious to have us meet "Allie," who was already named by her previous owner, and by all accounts was an absolute delight. She was normally sociable and loving, but was sadly suffering from separation anxiety from being taken away from her owner of three years, and she was now somewhat withdrawn. But Diane had a warm and patient heart, and I knew if anyone could restore Allie to happiness and contentment, **she** could.

Oscar and I couldn't wait to meet Allie, but an unexpected turn of events would put off our first meeting for several months. Little did I know then, that I wouldn't be seeing any relatives or friends for quite some time.

Destiny had other plans for Oscar and me!

Exciting News Arrives

In September, I received a grant to extend my research to a small base group affiliated with the University of Rhode Island that was located in southern Italy. I had to be on my way in five short days and my head was spinning with necessary preparations that had to be made quickly.

I would be studying the fish indigenous to that area in the Gulf of Salerno. Fish called the Pelagic, Mullet and Medfly. Oscar and I would stay in the town of Amalfi in the Province of Salerno.

Most of my family came from south of Rome in Sora, but I had two cousins, two aunts and one uncle who lived in Ravello which was a town very close to where we would be living and working. I was fluent in Italian and that would be a big help to everyone involved. I knew by the time we returned, Oscar would also understand many words in Italian!

I was so happy to be offered this opportunity and to travel to a location that I had been hearing my mother and father talk about for years. "This is too good to be true," I said to Oscar. "How would you like to go to Italy?" I'm pretty sure he nodded approvingly and of course that little smile was always there to let me know he was ready to pack his favorite toys and blankets at a moment's notice as soon as I would say, "Arrivederci Rhode Island!"

As Oscar and I began our second year together more adventures awaited us, but never in my wildest dreams could I imagine how far from the coastline of Rhode Island we would find ourselves; and how Oscar would become a famous celebrity in his travels.

Epilogue

Oscar and so many pets like him are capable of such loyalty and unconditional love that we can't even begin to imagine just how deep their devotion and allegiance goes.

We hear true stories of how dogs and cats travel thousands of miles to reunite with families from whom they were separated.

A recent movie gave the account of a dog who returned to the same spot near a railway station where he walked with his master every day for several years; and always came back later in the day to greet him upon his return. Until one day the owner didn't return because he had died before boarding the train to come home.

The dog continued to go back to the railway station every morning and every evening for the next ten years hoping his beloved master would return, but of course he never did.

The faithful dog died of old age at the railway station in a snow storm, and was found frozen in the snow by shop keepers the next morning.

A lovely memorial statue was erected where he died.

It is up to us to learn that there is a profound connection with our pet friends, and we are extremely blessed when they let us into their hearts.

You can always recognize a dog on the street who trusted

the wrong person and was betrayed with abuse or neglect. It is the dog with his head down walking in circles with no direction. It is the dog with the empty or sometimes anxious look on his face. These are the animals who have had their spirit broken by unkind humans. Some can be saved and restored, but others never can.

If we have an opportunity to adopt a dog or a cat, or any animal that would be entrusted into our care, it is our responsibility to look past their endearing features, and see that animal as a sensitive, feeling, caring and <u>thinking</u> creature just like ourselves… only that cannot speak. It can't say: "that hurts," "I'm hungry and thirsty," "I'm very cold," "please don't leave me in this hot car," or, "I really need to go outside, would you please take me out?" WE NEED TO HEAR WHAT THEY CAN'T SAY TO US

Questionnaire:

It is a privilege to own a pet, so before you think of bringing one home, please ask yourself three questions:

1. Can I be a good friend and know what my pet needs from me even though he can't tell me?

2. At the end of each day if my pet could talk would he say, "you were an excellent friend to me today?"

3. Will I always be kind and gentle with my pet as long as he lives?

If you give it a lot of thought, and answer all of these questions honestly with **"yes,"** then there is an amazing pet waiting just for you who will love you <u>forever</u>!

Oscar would say, "THANK YOU!"

Made in the USA
Lexington, KY
08 September 2015